Power
Quotes *

Power Quotes *

Unlocking New Levels of Faith in Christ

Farley Dunn

THREE SKILLET

POWER QUOTES: UNLOCKING NEW LEVELS OF FAITH IN CHRIST, Dunn, Farley.
1st ed.

◆♥◆ THREE SKILLET

www.ThreeSkilletPublishing.com

ISBN: 978-1-943189-76-2

Introduction

Each Power Quote becomes a dynamic connection between you and the spiritual authority of Heaven.

Pulled directly from inspirational messages posted daily on the MyChurchNotes website, these Power Quotes sum up the messages into powerful nuggets of truth.

Find the full articles containing each motivating and spirit-building Power Quote (plus more inspirational material) at www.MyChurchNotes.com or www.MyChurchNotes.net.

In addition to *Power Quotes: Unlocking New Levels of Faith in Christ*, look for these additional Power Quotes titles soon:

Power Quotes: Quotes to Release Your Spiritual Success

Power Quotes: Enabling Your Walk with Jesus

Power Quotes: Opening the Power of God's Word

Power Quotes: Revealing God's Path for Your Life

Each book contains 365 dynamic and spirit-engaging quotes, one for each day of the year. Get the set. You'll return to them again and again for the impact they make on your walk with Christ.

May this Spirit-empowered source of inspiration unlock a new level of relationship between you and God.

Farley Dunn

When God leads our adventure, we will find success at every turn.

From *"Our Great Adventure"*

Based on The Word of God as found in

1 Samuel 14:6

"Come, let us go over to the garrison of these uncircumcised. It may be that the Lord will work for us, for nothing can hinder the Lord from saving by many or by few."

Toss the prod and bring out the praise. It's much more effective.

From *"Putting Away the Cattle Prod"*

Based on The Word of God as found in

Ephesians 6:4

"Fathers, do not provoke your children to anger, but bring them up in the discipline and instruction of the Lord."

When God lays out a spread, every attendee can dine to his heart's content.

From *"Our JULY God"*

Based on The Word of God as found in

Acts 1:8

"But you will receive power when the Holy Spirit has come upon you, and you will be my witnesses in Jerusalem and in all Judea and Samaria, and to the end of the earth."

If we trade everything for the cross, the end has justified everything, and it will be worth it.

From *"The End Justifies the Means"*

Based on The Word of God as found in

1 Peter 4:19

"Therefore let those who suffer according to God's will entrust their souls to a faithful Creator while doing good."

Jesus' unseen hand is a magnet that draws us unto Him.

From *"The Dance of the Paperclip"*

Based on The Word of God as found in

John 12:32

"And I, when I am lifted up from the earth, will draw all people to myself."

There is no better pick-me-up than to spend our day with God.

From *"Our AIRY God"*

Based on The Word of God as found in

Psalm 45:17

"I will cause your name to be remembered in all generations; therefore nations will praise you forever and ever."

What is hidden will come to light. Let's make sure it's the saving hand of Jesus.

From *"Judge Judy"*

Based on The Word of God as found in

John 5:27

"And he has given him authority to execute judgment, because he is the Son of Man."

What we are around rubs off on us. Let's make sure we are covered with the Lord.

From *"A Sewer Stink"*

Based on The Word of God as found in

Genesis 19:3

"But he pressed them strongly; so they turned aside to him and entered his house. And he made them a feast and baked unleavened bread, and they ate."

8

We need to grab hold of the cross, for there is where our salvation is found.

From *"A Lawyer's Bane"*

Based on The Word of God as found in

Galatians 2:16

"We know that a person is not justified by works of the law but through faith in Jesus Christ."

When we develop in Christ, we start to look just like Him.

From *"The Photo Negative Effect"*

Based on The Word of God as found in

1 John 3:3

"And everyone who thus hopes in him purifies himself as he is pure."

To build for eternity, we need to let Jesus be our architect.

From *"Kingdom Ishmael"*

Based on The Word of God as found in

Deuteronomy 18:18

"I will raise up for them a prophet like you from among their brothers. And I will put my words in his mouth, and he shall speak to them all that I command him."

When we need encouragement, God will be there, and He will lift us above our problems.

From *"Our SPICE God"*

Based on The Word of God as found in

Numbers 6:25

"The Lord make his face to shine upon you and be gracious to you."

Jesus is our edge that allows us to overcome the temptations of the world.

From *"Our Edge on the World"*

Based on The Word of God as found in

1 John 1:9

"If we confess our sins, he is faithful and just to forgive us our sins and to cleanse us from all unrighteousness."

When we put aside all carnal behaviors, they become dead things to cast aside.

From *"Death to the Infidel"*

Based on The Word of God as found in

2 Timothy 2:22

"So flee youthful passions and pursue righteousness, faith, love, and peace, along with those who call on the Lord from a pure heart."

We are soldiers in the army of the Lord, and once a soldier draws a line, the battle becomes fully engaged.

From *"The Great Misconception"*

Based on The Word of God as found in

Ephesians 6:11

"Put on the whole armor of God, that you may be able to stand against the schemes of the devil."

15

When we stand by the Lord, He will proclaim our deliverance in the light of His blazing glory.

From *"A Billboard for All to Read"*

Based on The Word of God as found in

2 Kings 19:34

"For I will defend this city to save it, for my own sake and for the sake of my servant David."

God doesn't always ask us to understand. Sometimes He simply says no.

From *"Off-Limit Prayers"*

Based on The Word of God as found in

Luke 22:42

"Father, if you are willing, remove this cup from me. Nevertheless, not my will, but yours, be done."

Our faith in Christ writes us a check that can never be voided.

From *"Our Voided Check"*

Based on The Word of God as found in

Romans 4:14-15

"For if it is the adherents of the law who are to be the heirs, faith is null and the promise is void. For the law brings wrath, but where there is no law there is no transgression."

Jesus is the victor, and when we are on His side, we will gain all the glory.

From *"On the Winner's Side"*

Based on The Word of God as found in

Daniel 7:9

"The Ancient of Days took his seat; his clothing was white as snow, and the hair of his head like pure wool; his throne was fiery flames; its wheels were burning fire."

If God says it, we can write a check. The promise is already in the bank.

From *"Pressure Cooker Promises"*

Based on The Word of God as found in

2 Kings 8:19

"Yet the Lord was not willing to destroy Judah, for the sake of David his servant, since he promised to give a lamp to him and to his sons forever."

Even the forbidding poles of our world are no more than a cooling respite for the King who calls them His own.

From *"Our POLAR God"*

Based on The Word of God as found in

John 10:3

"To him the gatekeeper opens. The sheep hear his voice, and he calls his own sheep by name and leads them out."

When we choose Jesus, we've made the good choice.

From *"Good Cop, Bad Cop"*

Based on The Word of God as found in

Matthew 7:1-2

"Judge not, that you be not judged. For with the judgment you pronounce you will be judged, and with the measure you use it will be measured to you."

Once we learn to share, Jesus will use us to draw others to Him.

From *"The Houseguest"*

Based on The Word of God as found in

Luke 19:8

"And Zacchaeus stood and said to the Lord, 'Behold, Lord, the half of my goods I give to the poor. And if I have defrauded anyone of anything, I restore it fourfold.'"

God wants to rinse every bit of sin from our lives, so that we will stand clean and pure before Him.

From *"Rinsing the Dog"*

Based on The Word of God as found in

1 John 1:9

"If we confess our sins, he is faithful and just to forgive us our sins and to cleanse us from all unrighteousness."

When people see us live like Jesus, they will want to come to Jesus.

From *"Our Beautiful Adornments"*

Based on The Word of God as found in

Galatians 5:16

"But I say, walk by the Spirit, and you will not gratify the desires of the flesh."

Get ready. The flood of God's blessings is on the way.

From *"The Good Flood"*

Based on The Word of God as found in

Romans 15:13

"May the God of hope fill you with all joy and peace in believing, so that by the power of the Holy Spirit you may abound in hope."

When life takes everything from us, we can be assured we still have God.

From *"Abide the Fire"*

Based on The Word of God as found in

Jeremiah 23:29

"Is not my word like fire, declares the Lord, and like a hammer that breaks the rock in pieces?"

What we lift up before the Lord, He will make into something we never imagined possible.

From *"Lift Up the Lad"*

Based on The Word of God as found in

Genesis 21:18

"Up! Lift up the boy, and hold him fast with your hand, for I will make him into a great nation."

When we plant our roots in God, we will never falter in our walk with Him.

From *"Our FERTILE God"*

Based on The Word of God as found in

Psalm 19:9

"The fear of the Lord is clean, enduring forever; the rules of the Lord are true, and righteous altogether."

Let's make sure it's the honor of Christ that's reflected in our actions.

From *"The Wall of Honor"*

Based on The Word of God as found in

Colossians 1:25

"I became a minister according to the stewardship from God that was given to me for you, to make the word of God fully known."

If we want to know the true Jesus, all we have to do is read about Him in the Bible.

From *"Finding the Lost Jesus"*

Based on The Word of God as found in

2 Kings 8:19

"You search the Scriptures because you think that in them you have eternal life; and it is they that bear witness about me."

When we remember God's blessings, we are reminded of His love for us.

From *"Our Tally Marks"*

Based on The Word of God as found in

Revelation 1:19

"Write therefore the things that you have seen, those that are and those that are to take place after this."

32

When the world throws filth our way, we can look to Jesus, for His stains were the sign that His glory was on the way.

From *"A Tub Full of False Accusations"*

Based on The Word of God as found in

Luke 23:14

"You brought me this man as one who was misleading the people. And after examining him before you, behold, I did not find this man guilty of any of your charges against him."

When we come to God, we caress His heart with our presence, and He knows the joy of our love.

From *"The Knife Plunged Into Our Heart"*

Based on The Word of God as found in

Luke 22:44

"And being in agony he prayed more earnestly; and his sweat became like great drops of blood falling down to the ground."

Let's go for the sure thing. Let's invest in Jesus.

From *"Almost Saved"*

Based on The Word of God as found in

Matthew 7:3

"Why do you see the speck that is in your brother's eye, but do not notice the log that is in your own eye?"

The world surrounds us with fear, but Jesus fills us with peace.

From *"Life Without Fear"*

Based on The Word of God as found in

2 Peter 3:9

"The Lord is not slow to fulfill his promise as some count slowness, but is patient toward you, not wishing that any should perish, but that all should reach repentance."

When we emulate Jesus, we move from the realm of humanity into the realm of godliness.

From *"Becoming Like Jesus"*

Based on The Word of God as found in

John 1:12

"But to all who did receive him, who believed in his name, he gave the right to become children of God."

When we show love to one another, all our other problems will seem to melt into the background.

From *"Our FAN God"*

Based on The Word of God as found in

John 13:34

"A new commandment I give to you, that you love one another: just as I have loved you, you also are to love one another."

The next step for the Christian always involves leading others to salvation at the cross of Jesus.

From *"What Next?"*

Based on The Word of God as found in

Matthew 28:19-20

"Go therefore and make disciples of all nations, baptizing them in the name of the Father and of the Son and of the Holy Spirit, teaching them to observe all that I have commanded you."

39

When the world seems most barren is when we should search for Jesus the hardest.

From *"Under the Ice"*

Based on The Word of God as found in

Jeremiah 29:13

"You will seek me and find me, when you seek me with all your heart."

We cannot drift so far from God that He cannot find us, in order that He might call us back to Him.

From *"A Pain in the Neck"*

Based on The Word of God as found in

Jeremiah 1:9

"Then the Lord put out his hand and touched my mouth. And the Lord said to me, 'Behold, I have put my words in your mouth.'"

When we follow Jesus' commands, He will brag to the Father about us.

From *"Simon Says"*

Based on The Word of God as found in

Colossians 1:21-22

"You, who once were alienated and hostile in mind, doing evil deeds, he has now reconciled ... in order to present you holy and blameless and above reproach before him."

The greater our faith in Jesus, the greater the works He can do through us.

From *"Rolling in the Dough"*

Based on The Word of God as found in

Matthew 15:28

"Then Jesus answered her, 'O woman, great is your faith! Be it done for you as you desire.' And her daughter was healed instantly."

43

God rescues us from the world that besets us. We simply need to take Him at His word.

From *"Abandoning Our Sinking Ship"*

Based on The Word of God as found in

Job 17:2

"Surely there are mockers about me, and my eye dwells on their provocation."

When love lets us remain kind, we can know we are right where God wishes us to be.

From *"The Pincushion Heart"*

Based on The Word of God as found in

John 21:17

"He said to him the third time, 'Simon, son of John, do you love me?' Peter was grieved ... and he said to him, 'Lord, you know everything; you know that I love you.' Jesus said to him, 'Feed my sheep.'"

God cries "Silence!" to the cacophony of this world, in order that we may hear His still, small voice.

From *"God Cries, 'Silence!'"*

Based on The Word of God as found in

Habakkuk 2:20

"But the Lord is in his holy temple; let all the earth keep silence before him."

In order to choose life, we must walk in the footsteps of Jesus.

From *"A Surgeon's Choice"*

Based on The Word of God as found in

Romans 8:6

"For to set the mind on the flesh is death, but to set the mind on the Spirit is life and peace."

God is not tightfisted with us, and He expects us to be generous with what we have received.

From *"Sharing Our Windfall"*

Based on The Word of God as found in

Numbers 31:54

"Moses and Eleazar the priest received the gold from the commanders of thousands and of hundreds, and brought it into the tent of meeting, as a memorial for the people of Israel before the Lord."

God takes into account our flawed natures, and He continually draws us to Him.

From *"God's Spare Tire"*

Based on The Word of God as found in

Genesis 8:21

"And when the Lord smelled the pleasing aroma, the Lord said in his heart, 'I will never again curse the ground because of man.'"

God is only as far from us as we allow Him to be. All we must do is write His words on our hearts.

From *"Portrait of God"*

Based on The Word of God as found in

2 Samuel 22:2-3

"The Lord is my rock and my fortress and my deliverer, my God, my rock, in whom I take refuge, my shield, and the horn of my salvation, my stronghold and my refuge, my savior; you save me from violence."

50

God will make us champions, enabling us to do things we never thought possible.

From *"Our FRISBEE God"*

Based on The Word of God as found in

Psalm 27:1

"The Lord is my light and my salvation; whom shall I fear? The Lord is the stronghold of my life; of whom shall I be afraid?"

51

God will lift us up before the world, and His name will be shouted before all creation.

From *"God Will Lift Us Up"*

Based on The Word of God as found in

Romans 9:17

"For this very purpose I have raised you up, that I might show my power in you, and that my name might be proclaimed in all the earth."

Names may be used very differently today than they were in biblical times, but they still tell the world who we are.

From *"The Name Game (Part 1)"*

Based on The Word of God as found in

Proverbs 22:1

"A good name is to be chosen rather than great riches, and favor is better than silver or gold."

Jesus will find us in the depths of our despair, and He will never leave us.

From *"Five Steps to Success in Jesus"*

Based on The Word of God as found in

Acts 2:38

"And Peter said to them, 'Repent and be baptized every one of you in the name of Jesus Christ for the forgiveness of your sins, and you will receive the gift of the Holy Spirit.'"

Jesus is still the Truth, the Light, and the Way.

From *"Are You Out There, God? (Part 1)"*

Based on The Word of God as found in

Isaiah 40:3

"A voice cries: 'In the wilderness prepare the way of the Lord; make straight in the desert a highway for our God.'"

The land of milk and honey is found in the love we share with those around us. Let's be generous in sharing that love.

From *"Eight Maids-a-Milking"*

Based on The Word of God as found in

1 Corinthians 9:7

"Who serves as a soldier at his own expense? Who plants a vineyard without eating any of its fruit? Or who tends a flock without getting some of the milk?"

Window or aisle? Whichever we choose, we have to make sure we let God remain in control.

From *"Choosing the Window Seat"*

Based on The Word of God as found in

Matthew 26:42

"My Father, if this cannot pass unless I drink it, your will be done."

God is worth much more than a catfish or a dead octopus. He is worth our everlasting praise.

From *"Cast Your Octopus Before the Victor"*

Based on The Word of God as found in

Psalm 8:1

"O Lord, our Lord, how majestic is your name in all the earth! You have set your glory above the heavens."

All we need to do is look around us, and we will see the mighty hand of God.

From *"Our ACORN God"*

Based on The Word of God as found in

Ruth 1:16

"But Ruth said, 'Do not urge me to leave you or to return from following you. For where you go I will go, and where you lodge I will lodge. Your people shall be my people, and your God my God.'"

59

When we make a contract with God, there are never any hidden fees to come back and bite us.

From *"Hidden Fees"*

Based on The Word of God as found in

Genesis 27:33

"Then Isaac trembled very violently and said, 'Who was it then that hunted game and brought it to me, and I ate it all before you came, and I have blessed him? Yes, and he shall be blessed.'"

60

Our expiration date is in our minds. God only sees expectation dates for the job He wishes us to do.

From *"Our Expiration Date"*

Based on The Word of God as found in

Genesis 9:28

"After the flood Noah lived 350 years. All the days of Noah were 950 years, and he died."

God provides us a door of opportunity to do something grand for Him. It is up to us to step through.

From *"Does God Waste Our Time?"*

Based on The Word of God as found in

Matthew 24:44

"Therefore you also must be ready, for the Son of Man is coming at an hour you do not expect."

When we resolve our issues with one another, God will accept our praise and give us the desires of our hearts.

From *"Seven Things from God's Wishing Well (Part 7)"*

Based on The Word of God as found in

Matthew 5:23-24

"If you ... remember that your brother has something against you, leave your gift there before the altar and go. First be reconciled to your brother, and then come and offer your gift."

Christ nailed all our sins to the cross, and we are now alive in Him.

From *"Rekindled Love"*

Based on The Word of God as found in

Colossians 2:13

"And you, who were dead in your trespasses and the uncircumcision of your flesh, God made alive together with him, having forgiven us all our trespasses."

God wants us to worship Him in our spirit.

From *"Put On a New Robe"*

Based on The Word of God as found in

Psalm 95:6

"Oh come, let us worship and bow down; let us kneel before the Lord, our Maker!"

Jesus promises He will be with us in our darkest hours, and through Him, we will have a great reward.

From *"Blessed Are You When People Insult You..."*

Based on The Word of God as found in

Matthew 5:11

"Blessed are you when others revile you and persecute you and utter all kinds of evil against you falsely on my account."

Our beauty is found in our love for the needy, not in how we appear to those who stand afar off.

From *"Seven Swans-a-Swimming"*

Based on The Word of God as found in

Leviticus 11:13

"And these you shall detest among the birds; they shall not be eaten; they are detestable: the eagle, the bearded vulture, the black vulture."

When we wield the Bible's power, even the devil must fall to his knees.

From *"A Spiritual Texas"*

Based on The Word of God as found in

Exodus 22:2

"If a thief is found breaking in and is struck so that he dies, there shall be no bloodguilt for him."

God is our only fortification against every evil thing.

From *"The Foolish Pig"*

Based on The Word of God as found in

Jeremiah 49:32

"I will scatter to every wind those who cut the corners of their hair, and I will bring their calamity from every side of them, declares the Lord."

Our love for our Lord will be seen in the details of our daily walk with Him.

From *"Love Is in the Details"*

Based on The Word of God as found in

2 Timothy 4:9, 13

"Do your best to come to me soon. When you come, bring the cloak that I left with Carpus at Troas, also the books, and above all the parchments."

If we follow God's instructions for today, He will take care of our tomorrow.

From *"God's GPS"*

Based on The Word of God as found in

Acts 22:10

"And I said, 'What shall I do, Lord?' And the Lord said to me, 'Rise, and go into Damascus, and there you will be told all that is appointed for you to do.'"

Power Quotes
Unlocking New Levels of Faith in Christ

Our God both enables us and protects us, no matter where He sends us.

From *"Our SANDALS God"*

Based on The Word of God as found in

Acts 12:8

"And the angel said to him, 'Dress yourself and put on your sandals.' And he did so. And he said to him, 'Wrap your cloak around you and follow me.'"

When we respect our parents, God will shower us with the best in His storehouses.

From *"The Commandment with Promise"*

Based on The Word of God as found in

Exodus 20:12

"Honor your father and your mother, that your days may be long in the land that the Lord your God is giving you."

God wants us to bow before Him, for when we do, His love abounds.

From *"Seven Things from God's Wishing Well (Part 6)"*

Based on The Word of God as found in

1 John 5:14-15

"And this is the confidence that we have toward him, that if we ask anything according to his will he hears us. And if we know that he hears us in whatever we ask, we know that we have the requests that we have asked of him."

Death is found in the world, but to come to Christ is to find life anew.

From *"Our VERDANT God"*

Based on The Word of God as found in

Psalm 90:1

"Lord, you have been our dwelling place in all generations."

Our days are numbered, and God helps us make the best use of the time we've been given.

From *"Countdown to God"*

Based on The Word of God as found in

James 4:14

"Yet you do not know what tomorrow will bring. What is your life? For you are a mist that appears for a little time and then vanishes."

When we uphold God's moral standards, He will reward us with the kingdom of heaven.

From *"Blessed Are Those Who Are Persecuted..."*

Based on The Word of God as found in

Matthew 5:10

"Blessed are those who are persecuted for righteousness'
sake, for theirs is the kingdom of heaven."

When we labor together for Christ, there is nothing we cannot accomplish as a team.

From *"Six Geese-a-Laying"*

Based on The Word of God as found in

Genesis 1:20

"And God said, 'Let the waters swarm with swarms of living creatures, and let birds fly above the earth across the expanse of the heavens.'"

78

To trust in ourselves is to lose everything. To trust in Jesus is to become like Him.

From *"Almost Kings"*

Based on The Word of God as found in

1 Chronicles 11:10

"Now these are the chiefs of David's mighty men, who gave him strong support in his kingdom, together with all Israel, to make him king, according to the word of the Lord concerning Israel."

God's rewards are so great that our earthly dreams pale in comparison.

From *"Our HARVEST God"*

Based on The Word of God as found in

Isaiah 9:3

"You have multiplied the nation; you have increased its joy; they rejoice before you as with joy at the harvest, as they are glad when they divide the spoil."

God desires us to offer hope to the weary and life to the dying. God chooses life over death.

From *"Forsaken by God"*

Based on The Word of God as found in

2 Kings 21:13

"I will stretch over Jerusalem the measuring line of Samaria, and the plumb line of the house of Ahab, and I will wipe Jerusalem as one wipes a dish, wiping it and turning it upside down."

We live in the last days, and we must be ever vigilant that we do not stray from the teachings of Christ.

From *"Seven Danger Signs for the End Days"*

Based on The Word of God as found in

2 Timothy 3:2-4

"For people will be lovers of self, lovers of money, proud, arrogant, abusive, disobedient to their parents, ungrateful, unholy, heartless, unappeasable, slanderous, without self-control … rather than lovers of God."

People around us are watching. When they see us live for Jesus, they will know Jesus lives in us.

From *"Good Men Can Be Found in Bad Places"*

Based on The Word of God as found in

Acts 20:22

"And now, behold, I am going to Jerusalem, constrained by the Spirit, not knowing what will happen to me there."

When we embrace the world, we become like the world. When we embrace Jesus, we become like Him.

From *"A People Set Apart"*

Based on The Word of God as found in

Matthew 6:7-8

"And when you pray, do not heap up empty phrases as the Gentiles do, for they think that they will be heard for their many words. Do not be like them, for your Father knows what you need before you ask him."

When we are filled with the Holy Spirit, the Lord leads us in everything we do.

From *"The Day of Pentecost"*

Based on The Word of God as found in

Mark 16:17

"And these signs will accompany those who believe: in my name they will cast out demons; they will speak in new tongues."

When we encourage one another, and we follow God's instructions, He will bring us our victory.

From *"Fighting God's Fight"*

Based on The Word of God as found in

2 Timothy 1:7

"For God gave us a spirit not of fear but of power and love and self-control."

God wants to do a new thing in our life, but He can't if we're holding on to the past.

From *"God's New Thing (Part 2)"*

Based on The Word of God as found in

2 Chronicles 15:7

"But you, take courage! Do not let your hands be weak, for your work shall be rewarded."

God desires a reconciliation of the broken relationship between Him and His creation.

From *"Blessed Are the Peacemakers..."*

Based on The Word of God as found in

Matthew 5:9

"Blessed are the peacemakers, for they shall be called sons of God."

Jesus came in a manger that we might be one with the Father through Jesus the Son.

From *"Five Gold Rings"*

Based on The Word of God as found in

Exodus 39:21

"And they bound the breastpiece by its rings to the rings of the ephod with a lace of blue, ... that the breastpiece should not come loose from the ephod, as the Lord had commanded Moses."

God wishes us to draw unto him that He might become one with us.

From *"Split Eight Ways to Nothing"*

Based on The Word of God as found in

Jeremiah 50:5

"They shall ask the way to Zion, with faces turned toward it, saying, 'Come, let us join ourselves to the Lord in an everlasting covenant that will never be forgotten.'"

The presence of Christ makes our actions flavorful to those around us, and they will want to dine on Him.

From *"Needling the Cheese"*

Based on The Word of God as found in

Mark 9:50

"Salt is good, but if the salt has lost its saltiness, how will you make it salty again? Have salt in yourselves, and be at peace with one another."

The only true peace we can know comes from God alone.

From *"When God Gives Us Peace"*

Based on The Word of God as found in

1 Kings 21:25

"There was none who sold himself to do what was evil in the sight of the Lord like Ahab, whom Jezebel his wife incited."

The Father desires that no man should perish. He wishes all to come to Him by the way of his Son, Christ Jesus.

From *"He Plucks Us Out"*

Based on The Word of God as found in

Amos 4:11

"'I overthrew some of you, as when God overthrew Sodom and Gomorrah, and you were as a brand plucked out of the burning; yet you did not return to me,' declares the Lord."

When we follow the examples of the great leaders recorded in the Bible, we follow the example of Christ.

From *"Phone Call from God"*

Based on The Word of God as found in

2 Timothy 1:6-7

"For this reason I remind you to fan into flame the gift of God, which is in you through the laying on of my hands, for God gave us a spirit not of fear but of power and love and self-control."

We can run to Jesus, or we can run the other direction. Which will we choose?

From *"Which Will We Choose?"*

Based on The Word of God as found in

Joshua 24:15

"Choose this day whom you will serve, whether the gods your fathers served in the region beyond the River, or the gods of the Amorites in whose land you dwell. But as for me and my house, we will serve the Lord."

When God's presence washes over our lives, He brings the lushness of new life.

From *"Our LUSH God"*

Based on The Word of God as found in

Hebrews 2:18

"For because he himself has suffered when tempted, he is able to help those who are being tempted."

Maturity in Christ will lead us into eternal life, for we will become like Him.

From *"Repentance: Maturity in Christ"*

Based on The Word of God as found in

1 Corinthians 13:11

"When I was a child, I spoke like a child, I thought like a child, I reasoned like a child. When I became a man, I gave up childish ways."

97

If God is giving us ideas for the future, we must turn our backs on past mistakes.

From *"God's New Thing (Part 1)"*

Based on The Word of God as found in

Isaiah 43:18

"Remember not the former things, nor consider the things of old."

If we have a pure heart, our thoughts and intentions are unblemished by sin.

From *"Blessed Are the Pure in Heart..."*

Based on The Word of God as found in

Matthew 5:8

"Blessed are the pure in heart, for they shall see God."

When we follow Jesus, He will wipe all worry from our heart.

From *"Four Colly Birds"*

Based on The Word of God as found in

Solomon 2:12

"The flowers appear on the earth, the time of singing has come, and the voice of the turtledove is heard in our land."

Even when we are at our worst, God sees us at our best.

From *"The Payback We Deserve"*

Based on The Word of God as found in

Genesis 33:4

"But Esau ran to meet him and embraced him and fell on his neck and kissed him, and they wept."

Jesus came to leave us white as snow, a shining example of His love.

From *"The Dirty Rain"*

Based on The Word of God as found in

Leviticus 15:13

"And he shall bathe his body in fresh water and shall be clean."

102

God will lead us just where we need to go, and others will find redemption through us.

From *"Our Useless Mission"*

Based on The Word of God as found in

Joshua 2:1

"And Joshua the son of Nun sent two men secretly from Shittim as spies, saying, 'Go, view the land, especially Jericho.' And they went and came into the house of a prostitute whose name was Rahab and lodged there."

Our God expects us to love Him, but He makes sure we enjoy ourselves as we do.

From *"Our VACATION God"*

Based on The Word of God as found in

Psalm 98:5-6

"Sing praises to the Lord with the lyre, with the lyre and the sound of melody! With trumpets and the sound of the horn make a joyful noise before the King, the Lord!"

When the devil sends a storm against us, God simply allows the winds to carry us a new direction.

From *"When the Wind Comes"*

Based on The Word of God as found in

Acts 19:21

"Now after these events Paul resolved in the Spirit to pass through Macedonia and Achaia and go to Jerusalem, saying, 'After I have been there, I must also see Rome.'"

We have a direct feed to the greatest power source in all creation.

From *"Power from Praise"*

Based on The Word of God as found in

1 Chronicles 23:30

"And they were to stand every morning, thanking and praising the Lord, and likewise at evening."

When God asks things of us, it is only for our benefit, and He will reward us for wise decisions.

From *"Seven Things from God's Wishing Well (Part 5)"*

Based on The Word of God as found in

Deuteronomy 10:12-13

"What does the Lord your God require of you, but to fear the Lord your God, to walk in all his ways, to love him, to serve [him] ... and to keep the commandments and statutes of the Lord?"

The angels rejoice for spiritual victories that lead to eternal life in the kingdom of God.

From *"Repentance: The Heavens Rejoice"*

Based on The Word of God as found in

Luke 15:7

"Just so, I tell you, there will be more joy in heaven over one sinner who repents than over ninety-nine righteous persons who need no repentance."

If God is our focus, great material wealth will become a great opportunity to further His kingdom.

From *"Great Wealth"*

Based on The Word of God as found in

Luke 19:23

"Why then did you not put my money in the bank, and at my coming I might have collected it with interest?"

If we want to find Jesus in ourselves, look for Jesus in others, and soon Jesus will be all that people see in us.

From *"Blessed Are the Merciful..."*

Based on The Word of God as found in

Matthew 5:7

"Blessed are the merciful, for they shall receive mercy."

Our victory is assured, for the Christ is already the conqueror in the fight against sin.

From *"Three French Hens"*

Based on The Word of God as found in

Revelation 19:17

"Then I saw an angel standing in the sun, and with a loud voice he called to all the birds that fly directly overhead, 'Come, gather for the great supper of God.'"

God's blessings are all around us, and we need to recognize them for what they are.

From *"Our FOG God"*

Based on The Word of God as found in

Psalm 37:23

"The steps of a man are established by the Lord, when he delights in his way."

We risk disaster when we do not find our refuge in the Lord.

From *"The Earthquake that Shook a Nation"*

Based on The Word of God as found in

Acts 18:6

"He shook out his garments and said to them, 'Your blood be on your own heads! I am innocent. From now on I will go to the Gentiles.'"

We either learn God's lessons, or we are kicked onto the sidelines, as God leads His victors across the goal line.

From *"Famine 101"*

Based on The Word of God as found in

Jeremiah 14:2

"Judah mourns, and her gates languish; her people lament on the ground, and the cry of Jerusalem goes up."

When we remove our blinders, we see Jesus as He really is. He is our life and our salvation, and He draws us to him.

From *"With Blinded Eyes"*

Based on The Word of God as found in

John 10:32

"Jesus answered them, 'I have shown you many good works from the Father; for which of them are you going to stone me?'"

When God lays claim to us, not even the devil can make Him let go.

From *"Beloved Sons and Daughters"*

Based on The Word of God as found in

2 Timothy 1:2

"To Timothy, my beloved child: Grace, mercy, and peace from God the Father and Christ Jesus our Lord."

God gives us fathers to train us up to become strong watchtowers for the Lord.

From *"The Strong Towers"*

Based on The Word of God as found in

Genesis 18:19

"For I have chosen him, that he may command his children and his household after him to keep the way of the Lord by doing righteousness and justice, so that the Lord may bring to Abraham what he has promised him."

When the world takes everything we've got, God wants us to turn to Him.

From *"Seven Things from God's Wishing Well (Part 4)"*

Based on The Word of God as found in

James 1:5

"If any of you lacks wisdom, let him ask God, who gives generously to all without reproach, and it will be given him."

No matter how many times we fail God, He will continue to call us to repentance.

From *"Repentance: He Never Gives Up"*

Based on The Word of God as found in

Romans 11:29

"For the gifts and the calling of God are irrevocable."

When we follow Jesus' example, we will be offensive to no one.

From *"Two Turtle Doves"*

Based on The Word of God as found in

Matthew 10:42

"And whoever gives one of these little ones even a cup of cold water because he is a disciple, truly, I say to you, he will by no means lose his reward."

When the Lord speaks to us, we do well to listen to the sound of His voice.

From *"Have We Set God's Ring Tone?"*

Based on The Word of God as found in

Jeremiah 22:2

"Hear the word of the Lord, O king of Judah, who sits on the throne of David, you, and your servants, and your people who enter these gates."

God desires us to draw unto Him afresh, renewing our relationship once again.

From *"Blessings for Rent"*

Based on The Word of God as found in

Zechariah 8:9

"Let your hands be strong ... that the temple might be built."

Each level we reach only prepares us for the next course God intends for us to take.

From *"The Harder Test"*

Based on The Word of God as found in

1 Kings 17:22

"And the Lord listened to the voice of Elijah. And the life of the child came into him again, and he revived."

When God gives us a dose of His spit and polish, He uses His gentle love to make us new again.

From *"Spit and Polish"*

Based on The Word of God as found in

Hosea 2:20

"I will betroth you to me in faithfulness. And you shall know the Lord."

God has no patience with evildoers. Neither should we.

From *"Dividing the Truth"*

Based on The Word of God as found in

2 John 1:10

"If anyone comes to you and does not bring this teaching, do not receive him into your house or give him any greeting."

When we feel our lives are out of control, God is always in control.

From *"Our GYRO God"*

Based on The Word of God as found in

Acts 8:26

"Now an angel of the Lord said to Philip, 'Rise and go toward the south to the road that goes down from Jerusalem to Gaza.'"

God expects us to be His hand extended on earth.

From *"Seven Things from God's Wishing Well (Part 3)"*

Based on The Word of God as found in

Psalm 147:6

"The Lord lifts up the humble; he casts the wicked to the ground."

God is a loving father, and He sees our future glory, not our present failure.

From *"Repentance: That All May Come"*

Based on The Word of God as found in

2 Peter 3:9

"The Lord is not slow to fulfill his promise as some count slowness, but is patient toward you, not wishing that any should perish, but that all should reach repentance."

If we follow God's plan, we will become like Him, and the world will see Him in us.

From *"Salvation by Degree (Part 6)"*

Based on The Word of God as found in

2 Timothy 2:15

"Do your best to present yourself to God as one approved, a worker who has no need to be ashamed, rightly handling the word of truth."

When we are willing to set everything else aside to make room for the righteousness of God, He will give us satisfaction.

From *"Blessed Are Those Who Hunger and Thirst…"*

Based on The Word of God as found in

Matthew 5:6

"Blessed are those who hunger and thirst for righteousness, for they shall be satisfied."

When we cry unto Jesus, He brings us comfort in our time of need.

From *"A Partridge in a Pear Tree"*

Based on The Word of God as found in

1 Samuel 26:20

"Now therefore, let not my blood fall to the earth away from the presence of the Lord, for the king of Israel has come out to seek a single flea like one who hunts a partridge in the mountains."

Christians are known by the way they treat those trapped in the quagmire of the world.

From *"What Are Our Credentials?"*

Based on The Word of God as found in

Revelations 6:2

"And I looked, and behold, a white horse! And its rider had a bow, and a crown was given to him, and he came out conquering, and to conquer."

132

When we let Jesus fill up our lives, there is no room left for the devil to get inside.

From *"The Broken Man"*

Based on The Word of God as found in

Matthew 12:44-45

"And when [the unclean spirit] comes, it finds the house empty, swept, and put in order. Then it goes and brings with it seven other spirits more evil than itself ..."

God's love is in the gentle rain that comes after the storm.

From *"Our THUNDER God"*

Based on The Word of God as found in

Ezekiel 16:62

"I will establish my covenant with you, and you shall know that I am the Lord."

Even in our broken state, God treasures us, for He sees what we can become.

From *"Abandoned by God"*

Based on The Word of God as found in

Jeremiah 51:5

"For Israel and Judah have not been forsaken by their God, the Lord of hosts, but the land of the Chaldeans is full of guilt against the Holy One of Israel."

When we turn loose of all else to cling to Jesus, we keep the best of what God has in store for us.

From *"Keeping the Best"*

Based on The Word of God as found in

1 Samuel 15:3

"Now go and strike Amalek and devote to destruction all that they have. Do not spare them, but kill both man and woman, child and infant, ox and sheep, camel and donkey."

When the world sees Christ in us, they will know us for who we really are.

From *"His Banner Over Us"*

Based on The Word of God as found in

Solomon 6:10

"Who is this who looks down like the dawn, beautiful as the moon, bright as the sun, awesome as an army with banners?"

If we ask God for spiritual renewal, He will give us joy that no one can take from us.

From *"Seven Things from God's Wishing Well (Part 2)"*

Based on The Word of God as found in

Luke 11:10

"For everyone who asks receives, and the one who seeks finds, and to the one who knocks it will be opened."

When we pick up what God has asked us to turn loose of, He will be able to use it, and we will be filled with His power.

From *"Running on Autopilot"*

Based on The Word of God as found in

Exodus 3:10

"Come, I will send you to Pharaoh that you may bring my people, the children of Israel, out of Egypt."

When we give in to the love of God, He will instruct us on how we need to come to Him.

From *"Salvation by Degree (Part 5)"*

Based on The Word of God as found in

Romans 10:10

"For with the heart one believes and is justified, and with the mouth one confesses and is saved."

Jesus wishes us to champion those without hope, for then His kingdom will grow.

From *"Blessed Are the Meek..."*

Based on The Word of God as found in

Matthew 5:5

"Blessed are the meek, for they shall inherit the earth."

God has come in the person of Jesus, and He can live in our hearts today.

From *"A Plea from the Past"*

Based on The Word of God as found in

Psalm 7:1

"O Lord my God, in you do I take refuge; save me from all my pursuers and deliver me."

The only footsteps we can trust to lead us to the cross are those of Jesus.

From *"Where We Lead, They Shall Follow"*

Based on The Word of God as found in

Revelations 13:10

"If anyone is to be taken captive, to captivity he goes; if anyone is to be slain with the sword, with the sword must he be slain."

When our priorities are anywhere but on Jesus, our attention will be pulled away from Him.

From *"A Backpack and a Pocket of Change"*

Based on The Word of God as found in

Matthew 24:26-27

"If they say to you, 'Look, he is in the wilderness,' [or] 'Look, he is in the inner rooms,' do not believe it. For as the lightning comes from the east and shines as far as the west, so will be the coming of the Son of Man."

Our tears tell the world who we really are. Let's make sure they reveal Jesus in us.

From *"The World Weeps in Mourning"*

Based on The Word of God as found in

Revelation 18:10

"They will stand far off, in fear of her torment, and say, 'Alas! Alas! You great city, you mighty city, Babylon! For in a single hour your judgment has come.'"

Christ can make a difference in our lives when we have faith in Him.

From *"When Christ Has No Effect"*

Based on The Word of God as found in

Galatians 5:5

"For through the Spirit, by faith, we ourselves eagerly wait for the hope of righteousness."

There is none other so wise and good, and God deserves our praise.

From *"Our PICNIC God"*

Based on The Word of God as found in

1 Timothy 1:17

"To the King of the ages, immortal, invisible, the only God, be honor and glory forever and ever. Amen."

When we let God paint the picture, it will reflect His majesty and grace.

From *"God by the Numbers"*

Based on The Word of God as found in

Acts 9:5

"And [Saul] said, 'Who are you, Lord?' And he said, 'I am Jesus, whom you are persecuting.'"

When we align our hearts with God, the blessings we ask Him for will be the ones He intends to shower on us anyway.

From *"Seven Things from God's Wishing Well (Part 1)"*

Based on The Word of God as found in

Matthew 7:9

"Or which one of you, if his son asks him for bread, will give him a stone?"

Our God is ALIVE, and He rains life on us through His son, Jesus Christ.

From *"Our ALIVE God"*

Based on The Word of God as found in

1 Timothy 1:16

"But I received mercy for this reason, that in me, as the foremost, Jesus Christ might display his perfect patience as an example to those who were to believe in him for eternal life."

When we feel God's love and it becomes real to us, we want to turn from our sins and walk with Him.

From *"Salvation by Degree (Part 4)"*

Based on The Word of God as found in

Luke 15:32

"It was fitting to celebrate and be glad, for this your brother was dead, and is alive; he was lost, and is found."

When our hearts are broken over sin, we will know the full measure of God's comfort and blessing.

From *"Blessed Are Those Who Mourn..."*

Based on The Word of God as found in

Matthew 5:4

"Blessed are those who mourn, for they shall be comforted."

152

We are wise to remember that it doesn't do for God to have to tell us twice.

From *"Because I Said So"*

Based on The Word of God as found in

Revelation 16:19

"The great city was split into three parts, and the cities of the nations fell, and God remembered Babylon the great, to make her drain the cup of the wine of the fury of his wrath."

The only important thing people must find in us is Jesus.

From *"Picture Perfect"*

Based on The Word of God as found in

1 Corinthians 8:3

"But if anyone loves God, he is known by God."

God gives us His magnificent creation so that we will be reminded of Him.

From *"Our RED God"*

Based on The Word of God as found in

Psalm 97:1

"The Lord reigns, let the earth rejoice; let the many coastlands be glad!"

When we remember what God says, we have placed our feet on the road to salvation.

From *"The String Around God's Finger"*

Based on The Word of God as found in

1 Samuel 15:1

"And Samuel said to Saul, 'The Lord sent me to anoint you king over his people Israel; now therefore listen to the words of the Lord.'"

When we open God's Word, we have the source of wisdom in our hands.

From *"A Treasure Hunt"*

Based on The Word of God as found in

Proverbs 8:32

"And now, O sons, listen to me: blessed are those who keep my ways."

When we follow God's commands, He showers his blessings on us.

From *"God's Seven Blessings"*

Based on The Word of God as found in

Deuteronomy 28:1

"And if you faithfully obey the voice of the Lord your God, being careful to do all his commandments that I command you today, the Lord your God will set you high above all the nations of the earth."

What we do in ourselves can only be ordinary. What God does through us will be extraordinary.

From *"The Ordinary Becomes Extraordinary"*

Based on The Word of God as found in

Luke 6:19

"And all the crowd sought to touch him, for power came out from him and healed them all."

There is no greater name to bestow on a woman than that of Mother.

From *"Humanity's Greatest Achievement"*

Based on The Word of God as found in

Proverbs 31:28

"Her children rise up and call her blessed; her husband also, and he praises her."

When we allow God control, we will become like Him, and we will change people's lives.

From *"Repentance: Heart and Spirit"*

Based on The Word of God as found in

Mark 1:4

"John appeared, baptizing in the wilderness and proclaiming a baptism of repentance for the forgiveness of sins."

God loves us and continues to draw us to Him, even when we do not know Him.

From *"Salvation by Degree (Part 3)"*

Based on The Word of God as found in

1 Peter 1:8

"Though you have not seen him, you love him. Though you do not now see him, you believe in him and rejoice with joy that is inexpressible and filled with glory."

Jesus' purpose on earth had nothing to do with finances or earthly possessions. He came to fulfill the needs of our hearts.

From *"Blessed Are the Poor in Spirit..."*

Based on The Word of God as found in

Matthew 5:3

"Blessed are the poor in spirit, for theirs is the kingdom of heaven."

God desires us to be vessels of His power, so that others may be cleansed of their sins and their infirmities.

From *"The Cleansing Stone"*

Based on The Word of God as found in

Matthew 10:1

"He called to him his twelve disciples and gave them authority over unclean spirits, to cast them out, and to heal every disease and every affliction."

Our life becomes our legacy. It will continue to live and breathe long past when we are gone.

From *"Old Soldiers Never Die"*

Based on The Word of God as found in

2 Timothy 4:7

"I have fought the good fight, I have finished the race, I have kept the faith."

It is our faith, not our words or deeds, that draws Jesus unto us.

From *"The Woman Who Did a Man's Job"*

Based on The Word of God as found in

Mark 16:9

"Now when he rose early on the first day of the week, he appeared first to Mary Magdalene, from whom he had cast out seven demons."

Our rock is Jesus, and when we claim His righteousness, not even the devil can shake us free.

From *"The Destruction of the Great Towers"*

Based on The Word of God as found in

Isaiah 54:14

"In righteousness you shall be established; you shall be far from oppression, for you shall not fear; and from terror, for it shall not come near you."

When we take the time to read the directions, we will get our Christian walk right the first time.

From *"Have We Read the Directions?"*

Based on The Word of God as found in

2 Timothy 2:19

"But God's firm foundation stands, bearing this seal: 'The Lord knows those who are his,' and, 'Let everyone who names the name of the Lord depart from iniquity.'"

What the world sees as foolishness is really the triumphant hand of our Almighty God.

From *"The Third Hour of the Day"*

Based on The Word of God as found in

Acts 2:17

"And in the last days it shall be, God declares, that I will pour out my Spirit on all flesh, and your sons and your daughters shall prophesy, and your young men shall see visions, and your old men shall dream dreams."

If we keep our eyes on the prize, God will guide us safely home.

From *"Eyes on the Prize"*

Based on The Word of God as found in

Galatians 1:8

"But even if we or an angel from heaven should preach to you a gospel contrary to the one we preached to you, let him be accursed."

170

There is no darkness when we walk with God, for He shines with the light of His eternal glory.

From *"Our BRIGHT God"*

Based on The Word of God as found in

Psalm 19:1

"The heavens declare the glory of God, and the sky above proclaims his handiwork."

God is gentle and kind, His ways are above our ways, and for that, we can rejoice.

From *"Repentance: God-Given Sorrow"*

Based on The Word of God as found in

2 Corinthians 7:10

"For godly grief produces a repentance that leads to salvation without regret, whereas worldly grief produces death."

172

God knows what it's like to be human, and He continues to draw us to him.

From *"Salvation by Degree (Part 2)"*

Based on The Word of God as found in

1 Corinthians 6:19

"Or do you not know that your body is a temple of the Holy Spirit within you, whom you have from God? You are not your own."

When God gives us a revelation, we must follow His prompting and let Him bless us.

From *"Holding Success in Our Hands"*

Based on The Word of God as found in

2 Peter 1:3

"His divine power has granted to us all things that pertain to life and godliness, through the knowledge of him who called us to his own glory and excellence."

Jesus superseded everything that had come before Him. When we become like Him, He lifts us to stand at His side.

From *"Above the Law"*

Based on The Word of God as found in

John 1:17

"For the law was given through Moses; grace and truth came through Jesus Christ."

When God seems to have forgotten His promises to us, He is simply priming us for our victory lap.

From *"Primed for Our Season of Victory"*

Based on The Word of God as found in

1 Samuel 17:16

"For forty days the Philistine came forward and took his stand, morning and evening."

God wants His excellence to shine in everything we do, because that will draw others to Him.

From *"5-Star Jam"*

Based on The Word of God as found in

James 1:17-18

"Every good gift and every perfect gift is from . . . the Father of lights, with whom there is no variation or shadow . . . . Of his own will he brought us forth by the word of truth, that we should be a kind of firstfruits of his creatures."

When the evil one works his way into our lives, we must cut him out with the decisiveness of God's Word.

From *"The Head of the Snake"*

Based on The Word of God as found in

Joshua 11:10

"And Joshua turned back at that time and captured Hazor and struck its king with the sword, for Hazor formerly was the head of all those kingdoms."

There is no greater game than God's game, and the score- board is His to control.

From *"Our BASEBALL God"*

Based on The Word of God as found in

Psalm 40:3

"He put a new song in my mouth, a song of praise to our God. Many will see and fear, and put their trust in the Lord."

Let's invite God into our lives, for He will change our world for the better.

From *"Our Generation"*

Based on The Word of God as found in

Proverbs 30:32

"If you have been foolish, exalting yourself, or if you have been devising evil, put your hand on your mouth."

When we make a pinky promise with God, He will stand by our side, and the battle will be ours.

From *"God's Pinky Promise"*

Based on The Word of God as found in

Deuteronomy 29:1

"These are the words of the covenant that the Lord commanded Moses to make with the people of Israel in the land of Moab, besides the covenant that he had made with them at Horeb."

To find the best way to live, we need to see the world as God sees it.

From *"Making the Most of Our Lives (Part 2)"*

Based on The Word of God as found in

Romans 15:13

"May the God of hope fill you with all joy and peace in believing, so that by the power of the Holy Spirit you may abound in hope."

If we offer the hand of Christ's redemption, we must offer the other hand filled with kindness.

From *"Repentance: Hand in Hand"*

Based on The Word of God as found in

Luke 6:35

"But love your enemies, and do good, and lend, expecting nothing in return, and your reward will be great, and you will be sons of the Most High, for he is kind to the ungrateful and the evil."

183

God has a plan for us to move from death to life. He wants us to live an abundant life in Him.

From *"Salvation by Degree (Part 1)"*

Based on The Word of God as found in

Ecclesiastes 3:1

"For everything there is a season, and a time for every matter under heaven."

184

We should look at our life choices before we pray to God for healing.

From *"Dr. God"*

Based on The Word of God as found in

3 John 1:2

"Beloved, I pray that all may go well with you and that you may be in good health, as it goes well with your sou."

When we become shrink wrapped to one another in Jesus' name, we become stronger than if we stand alone.

From *"Shrink Wrapped for Jesus"*

Based on The Word of God as found in

1 Chronicles 12:1

"Now these are the men who came to David at Ziklag, while he could not move about freely because of Saul the son of Kish. And they were among the mighty men who helped him in war."

When man finds the truth that is in Christ, everyone who is hungry will be filled.

From *"Our MAIZE God"*

Based on The Word of God as found in

Ezra 3:11

"For he is good, for his steadfast love endures forever toward Israel."

When we stand with Jesus, His perfection covers all the mistakes we have ever made.

From *"The Best 21 Steps a Man Can Take"*

Based on The Word of God as found in

Job 31:6

"Let me be weighed in a just balance, and let God know my integrity!"

If we hold anything back, what we've held dear will get in the way of what the Lord wants us to accomplish.

From *"Emptying Our Pockets"*

Based on The Word of God as found in

2 Kings 12:2

"And Jehoash did what was right in the eyes of the Lord all his days, because Jehoiada the priest instructed him."

We are only free when we remain completely within the bounds of Christ.

From *"Freedom Without Bounds"*

Based on The Word of God as found in

John 8:32

"And you will know the truth, and the truth will set you free."

The two-faced person is a snake and a liar. God will cast him or her from our presence in exchange for our praise.

From *"The Person with Two Faces"*

Based on The Word of God as found in

Psalm 58:11

"Surely there is a reward for the righteous; surely there is a God who judges on earth."

In Christ, we are bound together under the covenant of God.

From *"A Covenant Broken"*

Based on The Word of God as found in

Galatians 4-7

"So you are no longer a slave, but a son, and if a son, then an heir through God."

It's our life. Let's throw out the dill pickles and live like we enjoy it!

From *"Making the Most of Our Lives (Part 1)"*

Based on The Word of God as found in

Psalms 25:12

"Who is the man who fears the Lord? Him will he instruct in the way that he should choose."

God looks past our social status, and He sees our spiritual status.

From *"Repentance: Pedigree Not Required"*

Based on The Word of God as found in

Acts 11:9

"But the voice answered a second time from heaven, 'What God has made clean, do not call common.'"

There is only one who can tame the mightiest of beasts: Jesus, through the blood He shed on the cross.

From *"The Mightiest of Beasts"*

Based on The Word of God as found in

James 3:7-8

"For every kind of beast and bird, of reptile and sea creature, can be tamed and has been tamed by mankind, but no human being can tame the tongue. It is a restless evil, full of deadly poison."

When we place our trust in God, we will find we need no other source of strength.

From *"The Headwaters of God"*

Based on The Word of God as found in

Zechariah 6:5

"And the angel answered and said to me, 'These are going out to the four winds of heaven, after presenting themselves before the Lord of all the earth.'"

The scales will fall from our eyes, and we will see that He is the Truth, the Light, and the only Way to eternal life.

From *"Three Blind Mice"*

Based on The Word of God as found in

2 Corinthians 13:3-4

"He is not weak in dealing with you, but is powerful among you. For he was crucified in weakness, but lives by the power of God. For we also are weak in him, but in dealing with you we will live with him by the power of God."

Our grandchildren should be the light of our lives, and we should ensure that God becomes the light of theirs.

From *"A Grandparent's Duty"*

Based on The Word of God as found in

Deuteronomy 4:9

"Only take care, and keep your soul diligently, lest you forget the things that your eyes have seen, and lest they depart from your heart all the days of your life. Make them known to your children and your children's children—"

God's Word shows us how to walk with Him in complete safety.

From *"Airbag Christianity"*

Based on The Word of God as found in

Matthew 6:24

"No one can serve two masters, for either he will hate the one and love the other, or he will be devoted to the one and despise the other. You cannot serve God and money."

Our actions reveal who Jesus is to those who have been blinded by sin.

From *"The Invisible Jesus"*

Based on The Word of God as found in

John 21:6

"He said to them, 'Cast the net on the right side of the boat, and you will find some.' So they cast it, and now they were not able to haul it in, because of the quantity of fish."

God is a mover and a shaker, and He is directly involved in our lives.

From *"Our ACTIVE God"*

Based on The Word of God as found in

Psalm 34:7

"The angel of the Lord encamps around those who fear him, and delivers them."

When we forgive those who have done us wrong, it is proof we are God's children.

From *"Forgiving the Unforgivable (Part 8)"*

Based on The Word of God as found in

Genesis 50:20

"As for you, you meant evil against me, but God meant it for good, to bring it about that many people should be kept alive, as they are today."

Through the eyes of Jesus, we can see people as they truly are.

From *"Repentance: Sinners Only Need Apply"*

Based on The Word of God as found in

Mark 2:16

"And the scribes of the Pharisees, when they saw that he was eating with sinners and tax collectors, said to his disciples, 'Why does he eat with tax collectors and sinners?'"

Whether God speaks with a whisper in the dark, or by moving the hands of kings, we are wise to listen.

From *"When God Calls..."*

Based on The Word of God as found in

Jeremiah 5:12

"They have spoken falsely of the Lord and have said, 'He will do nothing; no disaster will come upon us, nor shall we see sword or famine.'"

Jesus is our encourager and our eye of calm in the time of the storm.

From *"God's Encouraging Words"*

Based on The Word of God as found in

Galatians 6:9

"And let us not grow weary of doing good, for in due season
we will reap, if we do not give up."

When we dine on God, we become fat with His goodness and grace.

From *"Our YAM God"*

Based on The Word of God as found in

Ephesians 4:7

"But grace was given to each one of us according to the measure of Christ's gift."

When we dive into God's Word, we will bring nothing but beauty to the surface.

From *"Diving the Deep"*

Based on The Word of God as found in

Matthew 13:52

"And he said to them, 'Therefore every scribe who has been trained for the kingdom of heaven is like a master of a house, who brings out of his treasure what is new and what is old.'"

When God restores our lives, there is no remnant of the old man to be found.

From *"Broken Bones Restored"*

Based on The Word of God as found in

Jeremiah 50:19

"I will restore Israel to his pasture, and he shall feed on Carmel and in Bashan, and his desire shall be satisfied on the hills of Ephraim and in Gilead."

God's feast is already prepared. All we have to do is show up at the table.

From *"Our WATERMELON God"*

Based on The Word of God as found in

Romans 6:4

"We were buried therefore with him by baptism into death, in order that, just as Christ was raised from the dead by the glory of the Father, we too might walk in newness of life."

God's creation gives us reminders of His greatness. It is His way of drawing His children back to Him.

From *"The Sand Dollar Prayer"*

Based on The Word of God as found in

Psalm 50:14-15

"Offer to God a sacrifice of thanksgiving, and perform your vows to the Most High, and call upon me in the day of trouble; I will deliver you, and you shall glorify me."

When we quit turning to the Lord for guidance, we will quickly lose our way. Only God can lead us back home.

From *"A Gift of Lies"*

Based on The Word of God as found in

Joshua 9:14

"So the men took some of their provisions, but did not ask counsel from the Lord."

God only wants us to bring people to Him. Jesus will do the rest.

From *"Bring People to Jesus"*

Based on The Word of God as found in

John 12:21-22

"So these came to Philip, who was from Bethsaida in Galilee, and asked him, 'Sir, we wish to see Jesus.' Philip went and told Andrew; Andrew and Philip went and told Jesus."

When we bless them who persecute us, Jesus' light will shine through us.

From *"Forgiving the Unforgivable (Part 7)"*

Based on The Word of God as found in

Matthew 5:46

"For if you love those who love you, what reward do you have? Do not even the tax collectors do the same?"

When we ask according to God's will, He will give us the desires of our hearts.

From *"A Pocketbook God (Part 3)"*

Based on The Word of God as found in

1 John 5:14

"And this is the confidence that we have toward him, that if we ask anything according to his will he hears us."

The real meaning of a breakthrough is to find what God sees as important.

From *"Through God's Eyes"*

Based on The Word of God as found in

Psalms 89:34

"I will not violate my covenant or alter the word that went forth from my lips."

When we keep our eyes on Jesus, we will always reach the prize.

From *"A Fixed Point in Jesus"*

Based on The Word of God as found in

Mark 15:47

"Mary Magdalene and Mary the mother of [Joseph] saw where he was laid."

What we love, we share with the world. Let's make sure it's Jesus.

From *"Show and Tell"*

Based on The Word of God as found in

Mark 6:30

"The apostles returned to Jesus and told him all that they had done and taught."

When we go down clinging to Jesus, we come up again, stronger than before.

From *"Ducks in a Row"*

Based on The Word of God as found in

Luke 22:37

"For I tell you that this Scripture must be fulfilled in me: 'And he was numbered with the transgressors.' For what is written about me has its fulfillment."

218

Once we take life's biggest step, we will enrich ourselves with the rewards of our marital union every day.

From *"Life's Biggest Step"*

Based on The Word of God as found in

Genesis 2:18

"Then the Lord God said, 'It is not good that the man should be alone; I will make him a helper fit for him.'"

We either Trust or Bust, for with God there is no middle ground.

From *"Trust or Bust"*

Based on The Word of God as found in

Isaiah 26:19

"Your dead shall live; their bodies shall rise. You who dwell in the dust, awake and sing for joy!"

Jesus comes to us in the heat of the battle, and He provides just what we long for.

From *"Our ICE CREAM God"*

Based on The Word of God as found in

Deuteronomy 33:27

"The eternal God is your dwelling place, and underneath are the everlasting arms."

There is no going back on marriage. God will bless our union unto the end of days.

From *"As For Me and My House"*

Based on The Word of God as found in

Psalm 103:17

"But the steadfast love of the Lord is from everlasting to everlasting on those who fear him, and his righteousness to children's children."

When we understand how God sees our requests, we can expect Him to answer our prayers.

From *"A Pocketbook God (Part 2)"*

Based on The Word of God as found in

Zechariah 10:1

"Ask rain from the Lord in the season of the spring rain, from the Lord who makes the storm clouds, and he will give them showers of rain, to everyone the vegetation in the field."

What we do unto others, we also do unto God.

From *"Kindergarten's Life Lesson"*

Based on The Word of God as found in

1 Samuel 26:24

"Behold, as your life was precious this day in my sight, so may my life be precious in the sight of the Lord, and may he deliver me out of all tribulation."

God makes us new, and He wants us to remain without spot or wrinkle that we might worship Him.

From *"The Weight of Many Stones"*

Based on The Word of God as found in

Psalm 106:34-36

"They did not destroy the peoples, as the Lord commanded them, but they mixed with the nations and learned to do as they did. They served their idols, which became a snare to them."

All good things on the earth are God's, and He will shower His goodness on us.

From *"Our CIDER God"*

Based on The Word of God as found in

Zechariah 8:12

"For there shall be a sowing of peace. The vine shall give its fruit, and the ground shall give its produce, and the heavens shall give their dew. And I will cause the remnant of this people to possess all these things."

226

We can have the confidence that we know that we know that we know.

From *"At the Departure Gate"*

Based on The Word of God as found in

2 Timothy 4:8

"Henceforth there is laid up for me the crown of righteousness, which the Lord, the righteous judge, will award to me on that day, and not only to me but also to all who have loved his appearing."

227

Christ suffered first so that we would not be alone. He wishes us to be strong, as He was strong.

From *"Our Cross"*

Based on The Word of God as found in

2 Timothy 2:10

"Therefore I endure everything for the sake of the elect, that they also may obtain the salvation that is in Christ Jesus with eternal glory."

228

When doors shut in our faces, God has better doors for us to walk through.

From *"The Price of Purple"*

Based on The Word of God as found in

Acts 16:35

"But when it was day, the magistrates sent the police, saying, 'Let those men go.'"

When the world comes against us, God will show us opportunities to turn it around to our good.

From *"When the World Gives Evil for Good"*

Based on The Word of God as found in

Acts 3:13

"The God of Abraham, the God of Isaac, and the God of Jacob, the God of our fathers, glorified his servant Jesus, whom you delivered over and denied in the presence of Pilate, when he had decided to release him."

The Lord will bless us socially and financially, for He loves His children.

From *"The Gift of Work"*

Based on The Word of God as found in

Colossians 3:23-24

"Whatever you do, work heartily, as for the Lord and not for men, knowing that from the Lord you will receive the inheritance as your reward. You are serving the Lord Christ."

Only God can delete our sins from the record book. We repent, and He smiles on us once again.

From *"Repentance: Our Sins Remembered"*

Based on The Word of God as found in

Hosea 14:4

"I will heal their apostasy; I will love them freely, for my anger has turned from them."

God lifts us from the mud, and He carries us to the other side.

From *"Our GALOSHES God"*

Based on The Word of God as found in

Psalm 3:3

"But you, O Lord, are a shield about me, my glory, and the lifter of my head."

God understands our frailties. All we have to do is ask for His help.

From *"A Pocketbook Good (Part 3)"*

Based on The Word of God as found in

Genesis 32:29

"Then Jacob asked him, 'Please tell me your name.' But he said, 'Why is it that you ask my name?' And there he blessed him."

God is the essence of Truth, and He expects us to reflect Him to the world.

From *"Fire!"*

Based on The Word of God as found in

Ezekiel 13:13

"Therefore thus says the Lord God: I will make a stormy wind break out in my wrath, and there shall be a deluge of rain in my anger, and great hailstones in wrath to make a full end."

Jesus died on the cross to set us free. He whom Christ has set free is free indeed.

From *"The Iron Mask"*

Based on The Word of God as found in

Genesis 6:8

"But Noah found favor in the eyes of the Lord."

God is the Master Chef, and He creates good things for those that love Him.

From *"Chef's Delight"*

Based on The Word of God as found in

2 Chronicles 36:23

"Thus says Cyrus king of Persia, 'The Lord, the God of heaven ... has charged me to build him a house at Jerusalem, which is in Judah. Whoever is among you of all his people, ... let him go up.'"

237

Choosing Jesus doesn't mean giving up everything else. Rather, we allow God to take first place.

From *"Jesus on the Flip Side"*

Based on The Word of God as found in

Luke 18:29-30

"Truly, I say to you, there is no one who has left house or wife or brothers or parents or children, for the sake of the kingdom of God, who will not receive many times more in this time, and in the age to come eternal life."

238

During our days we wear many hats, but the most important hat is the one that belongs to Christ.

From *"Wearing Our Christ Hat"*

Based on The Word of God as found in

Romans 8:5

"For those who live according to the flesh set their minds on the things of the flesh, but those who live according to the Spirit set their minds on the things of the Spirit."

239

When we lift our voices in praise, the Father goes into battle before us and gives us the victory.

From *"Priming God's War Machine"*

Based on The Word of God as found in

2 Chronicles 20:22

"And when they began to sing and praise, the Lord set an ambush against the men of Ammon, Moab, and Mount Seir, who had come against Judah, so that they were routed."

240

God deserves our praise each and every moment of each and every day.

From *"Five Opportunities to Praise God"*

Based on The Word of God as found in

1 Chronicles 16:4

"Then he appointed some of the Levites as ministers before the ark of the Lord, to invoke, to thank, and to praise the Lord, the God of Israel."

If we allow God to rule our lives, the world will know that He is God.

From *"Making God's Mark"*

Based on The Word of God as found in

Mark 12:30

"And you shall love the Lord your God with all your heart and with all your soul and with all your mind and with all your strength."

If God is first in our life, we will offer Him the first fruits of all we have.

From *"Mirror, Mirror"*

Based on The Word of God as found in

Deuteronomy 17:1

"You shall not sacrifice to the Lord your God an ox or a sheep in which is a blemish, any defect whatever, for that is an abomination to the Lord your God."

243

Salvation through Jesus allows us to become what God really wants us to be.

From *"Cracked Like an Egg"*

Based on The Word of God as found in

Romans 2:15

"They show that the work of the law is written on their hearts, while their conscience also bears witness, and their conflicting thoughts accuse or even excuse them."

Building a strong foundation in good weather is what helps us survive the bad.

From *"The Keeper of the Light"*

Based on The Word of God as found in

1 John 2:28

"And now, little children, abide in him, so that when he appears we may have confidence and not shrink from him in shame at his coming."

All things work together for good even when all we can see is the betrayal that cuts our feet from under us.

From *"The Betrayal that Caused a Betrothal"*

Based on The Word of God as found in

John 18:1-2

"When Jesus had spoken these words, he went out with his disciples [to] a garden, which he and his disciples entered. Now Judas, who betrayed him, also knew the place, for Jesus often met there with his disciples."

246

When we feel we've lost God, we cry unto Him, and He proves Himself to us again.

From *"The Long Day"*

Based on The Word of God as found in

2 Kings 20:10

"And Hezekiah answered, 'It is an easy thing for the shadow to lengthen ten steps. Rather let the shadow go back ten steps.'"

There is only one God, and He drowns out the vile murmurs of the evil one.

From *"Our HOT God"*

Based on The Word of God as found in

Psalm 77:18

"The crash of your thunder was in the whirlwind; your lightnings lighted up the world; the earth trembled and shook."

Jesus is our power source. We will reside in the eternal light of His everlasting love.

From *"When the Lights Go Out"*

Based on The Word of God as found in

Luke 11:36

"If then your whole body is full of light, having no part dark, it will be wholly bright, as when a lamp with its rays gives you light."

Having a Savior who has our future in His hands is worth everything.

From *"The Story God Wrote"*

Based on The Word of God as found in

Mark 16:15-16

"And he said to them, 'Go into all the world and proclaim the gospel to the whole creation. Whoever believes and is baptized will be saved, but whoever does not believe will be condemned.'"

If we take away someone's good name, we've taken the most important thing they possess.

From *"Forgiving the Unforgivable (Part 5)"*

Based on The Word of God as found in

Genesis 43:34

"Portions were taken to them from Joseph's table, but Benjamin's portion was five times as much as any of theirs. And they drank and were merry with him."

When we pay God's blessings forward, we can be trusted with the bounty of His love.

From *"Pay It Forward"*

Based on The Word of God as found in

Deuteronomy 12:18

"You shall eat them before the Lord your God in the place that the Lord your God will choose, you and your son and your daughter, your male servant and your female servant, and the Levite who is within your towns."

The Lord is always something we can gossip about, for when we share the Lord, we share His love.

From *"The Good Gossip"*

Based on The Word of God as found in

Luke 1:58

"And her neighbors and relatives heard that the Lord had shown great mercy to her, and they rejoiced with her."

When we give Jesus what we cannot keep, He becomes the one thing we can hold to forever.

From *"What We Cannot Keep"*

Based on The Word of God as found in

John 21:18

"Truly, truly, I say to you, when you were young, you used to dress yourself and walk wherever you wanted, but when you are old, you will stretch out your hands, and another will dress you and carry you where you do not want to go."

Even as the world tries to thrash us into submission, we can depend on our God to be the rock to which we can cling.

From *"Our AUTUMNAL God"*

Based on The Word of God as found in

Mark 13:27

"And then he will send out the angels and gather his elect from the four winds, from the ends of the earth to the ends of heaven."

255

God draws the comic strip, and the devil runs when God tells him to.

From *"A Cartoon Catastrophe"*

Based on The Word of God as found in

Jeremiah 49:38

"And I will set my throne in Elam and destroy their king and officials, declares the Lord."

God wants us to kick back on Labor Day. Let's just not forget to make Him a part of our celebrations.

From *"The Worker Is Worthy of His Hire"*

Based on The Word of God as found in

Exodus 23:12

"Six days you shall do your work, but on the seventh day you shall rest; that your ox and your donkey may have rest, and the son of your servant woman, and the alien, may be refreshed."

It's the final touchdown that takes the game, but the victory in Christ is earned a single quarter at a time.

From *"Our Touchdown Dance"*

Based on The Word of God as found in

1 Peter 4:1

"Since therefore Christ suffered in the flesh, arm yourselves with the same way of thinking, for whoever has suffered in the flesh has ceased from sin."

Blood might be thicker than water, but the power of God trumps everything.

From *"Blood and Water"*

Based on The Word of God as found in

Matthew 19:6

"So they are no longer two but one flesh. What therefore God has joined together, let not man separate."

Jesus touched those broken and hurting, because that opened the way for them to come to Him.

From *"Heart Knowledge"*

Based on The Word of God as found in

Mark 10:52

"And Jesus said to him, 'Go your way; your faith has made you well.' And immediately he recovered his sight and followed him on the way."

260

When someone has done us wrong, and we have forgiven them, only two people need to know. Jesus and us.

From *"Forgiving the Unforgivable (Part 4)"*

Based on The Word of God as found in

Psalm 142:1-2

"With my voice I cry out to the Lord; with my voice I plea for mercy to the Lord. I pour out my complaint before him; I tell my trouble before him."

The knowledge of the Word can give us the traction control to follow God wherever He leads.

From *"The Traction Control Christian"*

Based on The Word of God as found in

Ephesians 4:23

"Be renewed in the spirit of your minds."

There is no limit to what we can do with Christ, but without Him, we cannot survive what the devil will bring against us.

From *"Childlike Faith"*

Based on The Word of God as found in

Jeremiah 17:5

"Thus says the Lord: 'Cursed is the man who trusts in man and makes flesh his strength, whose heart turns away from the Lord.'"

It is only when we are attached to the Father that we can feed on His life-giving power.

From *"The Withered Hand of God"*

Based on The Word of God as found in

Micah 3:4

"Then they will cry to the Lord, but he will not answer them; he will hide his face from them at that time, because they have made their deeds evil."

When we allow ourselves to be lifted up, we are held in the hands of the Father.

From *"The Needle of Pride"*

Based on The Word of God as found in

Genesis 49:18

"I wait for your salvation, O Lord."

We are to reflect the example of Christ found in the Scriptures.

From "*God's Finger*"

Based on The Word of God as found in

2 Timothy 4:5

"As for you, always be sober-minded, endure suffering, do the work of an evangelist, fulfill your ministry."

God provides a battle plan to restore us once again.

From *"He Will Restore Us Once Again"*

Based on The Word of God as found in

Jeremiah 50:18

"Therefore, thus says the Lord of hosts, the God of Israel: Behold, I am bringing punishment on the king of Babylon and his land, as I punished the king of Assyria."

When we come to the Father through Jesus, we can trust His redeeming grace to justify us as we stand before His throne.

From *"We Can Know That We Know"*

Based on The Word of God as found in

1 Corinthians 6:11

"But you were washed, you were sanctified, you were justified in the name of the Lord Jesus Christ and by the Spirit of our God."

When we feel life has shaken our soul, the peace of God can be ours.

From *"Our GENTLE God"*

Based on The Word of God as found in

Solomon 5:16

"His mouth is most sweet, and he is altogether desirable. This is my beloved and this is my friend, O daughters of Jerusalem."

When a wrong has been done against us, we must turn loose of our desire to take revenge.

From *"Forgiving the Unforgivable (Part 3)"*

Based on The Word of God as found in

Genesis 41:25, 32

"Then Joseph said to Pharaoh, 'The dreams of Pharaoh are one; God has revealed to Pharaoh what he is about to do. And the doubling of Pharaoh's dream means that the thing is fixed by God, and God will shortly bring it about.'"

270

To draw to God is to become wise. To withdraw from Him is to become a fool.

From *"A Foolish Life"*

Based on The Word of God as found in

Psalms 14:1

"The fool says in his heart, 'There is no God.' They are corrupt, they do abominable deeds; there is none who does good."

When we see only the cold rain and the mud, God changes the rain to snow, and the world becomes a beautiful place.

From *"A Few Degrees of Grace"*

Based on The Word of God as found in

Matthew 21:42

"The stone that the builders rejected has become the cornerstone; this was the Lord's doing, and it is marvelous in our eyes."

We are responsible to bring our children up to be the leaders God needs them to be.

From *"The Children of God Tomorrow"*

Based on The Word of God as found in

1 Thessalonians 5:5

"For you are all children of light, children of the day. We are not of the night or of the darkness."

When Christ offers us forgiveness, how can we not do the same for those around us?

From *"Offering Forgiveness"*

Based on The Word of God as found in

Galatians 4:14

"And though my condition was a trial to you, you did not scorn or despise me, but received me as an angel of God, as Christ Jesus."

When we trust in ourselves, we will fail. In God, we'll know success in Christ.

From *"Warning Signs"*

Based on The Word of God as found in

Proverbs 1:30

"[They] would have none of my counsel and despised all my reproof."

When our hearts are filled with Christ, the rest of us will become twice as nice.

From *"The Oddball Christian"*

Based on The Word of God as found in

Matthew 18:10

"See that you do not despise one of these little ones. For I tell you that in heaven their angels always see the face of my Father who is in heaven."

The consequences we want are the blessings that flow from the throne above.

From *"The Price of Food"*

Based on The Word of God as found in

Proverbs 6:30-31

"People do not despise a thief if he steals to satisfy his appetite when he is hungry, but if he is caught, he will pay sevenfold; he will give all the goods of his house."

With the Word of God, we can smash the evil one into dust that blows in the wind.

From *"Our Powerless Oppressor"*

Based on The Word of God as found in

Romans 8:37

"No, in all these things we are more than conquerors through him who loved us."

We have God's alarm clock. Why would we pay attention to the devil's snooze button?

From *"The Devil's Snooze Button"*

Based on The Word of God as found in

Matthew 24:42

"Therefore, stay awake, for you do not know on what day your Lord is coming."

When we taste the salvation of Jesus, we've eaten of the true bread of life.

From *"The True Bread"*

Based on The Word of God as found in

John 6:32

"Jesus then said to them, 'Truly, truly, I say to you, it was not Moses who gave you the bread from heaven, but my Father gives you the true bread from heaven.'"

Taking a break to recharge our energy makes us better Christians.

From *"Jesus' Chill Pill"*

Based on The Word of God as found in

Mark 6:31

"And he said to them, 'Come away by yourselves to a desolate place and rest a while.' For many were coming and going, and they had no leisure even to eat."

Jesus makes life better, when we decide that He's our number one goal in life.

From *"Our Good Attitude"*

Based on The Word of God as found in

Luke 10:42

"But one thing is necessary. Mary has chosen the good portion, which will not be taken away from her."

The softer we whisper of Christ, the more people will draw close to hear what we have to say.

From *"Overburdening Christ"*

Based on The Word of God as found in

Mark 1:45

"But he went out and began to talk freely about it, and to spread the news, so that Jesus could no longer openly enter a town, but was out in desolate places, and people were coming to him from every quarter."

283

When we place our faith in God, we open our eyes to the truth that there is no other Savior except Jesus, our Lord.

From *"The Pretenders"*

Based on The Word of God as found in

Matthew 24:27

"For as the lightning comes from the east and shines as far as the west, so will be the coming of the Son of Man."

When we look away from the hustle-bustle, we'll discover God in the quiet moments of our day.

From *"Three Days Into the Desert"*

Based on The Word of God as found in

Exodus 5:3

"Then they said, 'The God of the Hebrews has met with us. Please let us go a three days' journey into the wilderness that we may sacrifice to the Lord our God, lest he fall upon us with pestilence or with the sword.'"

The auction has already begun. If we want to join in and claim the prize of salvation, we need to speak up, please.

From *"Speak Up, Please"*

Based on The Word of God as found in

Romans 10:13

"For everyone who calls on the name of the Lord will be saved."

Even a foot outside Christ's will robs us of the beauty He desires to gift unto us.

From *"A Moment to Eclipse All Others"*

Based on The Word of God as found in

Ephesians 3:14-15

"For this reason I bow my knees before the Father, from whom every family in heaven and on earth is named."

God already knows our desires. When we place them before Him, He expected them all along.

From *"Placing Our Desires Before God"*

Based on The Word of God as found in

Joshua 18:8

"So the men arose and went, and Joshua charged those who went to write the description of the land, saying, 'Go . . . in the land and write a description and return to me. And I will cast lots for you here before the Lord in Shiloh.'"

In God we are rescued and have become mighty men and women of valor.

From *"God Lifts Us Up"*

Based on The Word of God as found in

Psalm 34:17

"When the righteous cry for help, the Lord hears and delivers them out of all their troubles."

Jesus has power over the devil, and when we become like Christ, so do we.

From *"Portrait of Humanity"*

Based on The Word of God as found in

Hebrews 2:14

"Since therefore the children share in flesh and blood, he himself likewise partook of the same things, that through death he might destroy the one who has the power of death, that is, the devil."

290

It's always Christ above us in every situation.

From *"Taking Care with the Cross"*

Based on The Word of God as found in

2 Peter 2:19

"They promise them freedom, but they themselves are slaves of corruption. For whatever overcomes a person, to that he is enslaved."

Jesus is our reason to rejoice, for in Him, we are eternally redeemed from sin and death.

From *"The Jesus Celebration"*

Based on The Word of God as found in

Luke 19:40

"He answered, 'I tell you, if these were silent, the very stones would cry out.'"

When we make a point to celebrate Jesus, soon Jesus will be the reason we want to celebrate.

From *"Our Moment of Revelation"*

Based on The Word of God as found in

Matthew 3:16

"And when Jesus was baptized, immediately he went up from the water, and behold, the heavens were opened to him, and he saw the Spirit of God descending like a dove and coming to rest on him."

When we clean up for Christ, the world will admire what we've become.

From *"Our Perfect Example"*

Based on The Word of God as found in

1 Timothy 4:12

"Let no one despise you for your youth, but set the believers an example in speech, in conduct, in love, in faith, in purity."

When God returns for His own, the bling of the world will fade into tattered rags.

From *"The Great City"*

Based on The Word of God as found in

Revelation 21:10-11

"And he carried me away in the Spirit to a great, high mountain, and showed me the holy city Jerusalem coming down out of heaven from God, having the glory of God, its radiance … like a jasper, clear as crystal."

When God instructs us, let's not hesitate. He's got something good waiting at the end.

From *"God's New Direction"*

Based on The Word of God as found in

Acts 10:13-14

"And there came a voice to him: 'Rise, Peter; kill and eat.'
But Peter said, 'By no means, Lord; for I have never eaten
anything that is common or unclean.'"

In Jesus, we find meaning in every single day.

From *"Sense Out of the Senseless"*

Based on The Word of God as found in

1 Corinthians 1:18

"For the word of the cross is folly to those who are perishing, but to us who are being saved it is the power of God."

Our ministry flows from us because others need the love of Jesus to pour from our hands.

From *"Jesus' Private Sorrow"*

Based on The Word of God as found in

Matthew 14:13

"Now when Jesus heard this, he withdrew from there in a boat to a desolate place by himself. But when the crowds heard it, they followed him on foot from the towns."

When we exercise our authority over this world with care, God will view our relation-ship with Him with a gentle eye.

From *"Turning Loose of the Reins"*

Based on The Word of God as found in

Romans 13:1

"Let every person be subject to the governing authorities. For there is no authority except from God, and those that exist have been instituted by God."

What manner of love is this that He should die for us?

From *"God Is Love"*

Based on The Word of God as found in

John 15:9

"As the Father has loved me, so have I loved you. Abide in my love."

The true test of our faith is when the storms of life smash into us. On Christ, our footing will be secure.

From *"Of Rock and Word"*

Based on The Word of God as found in

Matthew 7:25

"And the rain fell, and the floods came, and the winds blew and beat on that house, but it did not fall, because it had been founded on the rock."

When God opens a door, we must find it in ourselves to trust Him and step through.

From *"A Measure of Trust"*

Based on The Word of God as found in

Acts 11:5

"In a trance I saw a vision, something like a great sheet descending, being let down from heaven by its four corners, and it came down to me."

Our responsibility is to love, both in our relationship with God and with those at our side.

From *"Our Love Responsibility"*

Based on The Word of God as found in

Romans 14:19

"So then let us pursue what makes for peace and for mutual upbuilding."

God delights in us. He wants us to delight in Him.

From *"Getting Cool with God"*

Based on The Word of God as found in

Psalm 18:19

"He brought me out into a broad place; he rescued me, because he delighted in me."

Jesus carries the power of God in His fist and understands the frailty of humanity in His heart.

From *"Drawing Jesus"*

Based on The Word of God as found in

John 1:14

"And the Word became flesh and dwelt among us, and we have seen his glory, glory as of the only Son from the Father, full of grace and truth."

Let's trust in Christ and the cross instead of the world and its wastrels.

From *"Promises Unfulfilled"*

Based on The Word of God as found in

James 3:15

"This is not the wisdom that comes down from above, but is earthly, unspiritual, demonic."

Let's be gung-ho about Christ, for it's our life in Him that really matters.

From *"Mission Completed"*

Based on The Word of God as found in

Ephesians 4:7

"But grace was given to each one of us according to the measure of Christ's gift."

Jesus is our ladder set up on the earth, and He guides us to the heavenly Father above.

From *"Our Dreams of Christ"*

Based on The Word of God as found in

Genesis 28:13

"And behold, the Lord stood above [the ladder] and said, 'I am the Lord, the God of Abraham your father and the God of Isaac. The land on which you lie I will give to you and to your offspring.'"

When we wield the Word in the name of Christ, the victory will be ours.

From *"Rotten Fruit"*

Based on The Word of God as found in

Acts 13:12

"Then the proconsul believed, when he saw what had occurred, for he was astonished at the teaching of the Lord."

Following Jesus' example allows happiness to flow into our lives.

From *"As We Are in Christ"*

Based on The Word of God as found in

Luke 3:22

"The Holy Spirit descended on him in bodily form, like a dove; and a voice came from heaven, 'You are my beloved Son; with you I am well pleased.'"

When we're no longer afraid, we can become the warriors God wishes us to be.

From *"The Earth Shall Quake"*

Based on The Word of God as found in

Psalm 91:11

"For he will command his angels concerning you to guard you in all your ways."

311

When we want off the bottom rung of the ladder, we need to get with Jesus. He's at the top, and He wants us with him.

From *"The One Righteous God"*

Based on The Word of God as found in

Proverbs 30:4

"Who has ascended to heaven and come down? Who has gathered the wind in his fists? Who has wrapped up the waters in a garment? Who has established all the ends of the earth? What is his name, and what is his son's name?"

312

When we offer Christ our strengths, our weaknesses become small.

From *"Team Players in Christ"*

Based on The Word of God as found in

Psalm 133:1

"Behold, how good and pleasant it is when brothers dwell in unity!"

When we want to be like the Father, we must let Him be our new foundation.

From *"God's Remodeling Plan"*

Based on The Word of God as found in

Deuteronomy 9:21

"Then I took the sinful thing, the calf that you had made, and burned it with fire and crushed it, grinding it very small, until it was as fine as dust. And I threw the dust of it into the brook that ran down from the mountain."

The closer we get to God, the safer we are from the spiritual battles that will try to bring us down.

From *"The Furnace of the Lord"*

Based on The Word of God as found in

Exodus 19:18

"Now Mount Sinai was wrapped in smoke because the Lord had descended on it in fire. The smoke of it went up like the smoke of a kiln, and the whole mountain trembled greatly."

315

When our hand is in the hand of Christ, He will guide us to our ultimate reward.

From *"The Ultimate Reward"*

Based on The Word of God as found in

1 Thessalonians 4:16

"For the Lord himself will descend from heaven with a cry of command, with the voice of an archangel, and with the sound of the trumpet of God. And the dead in Christ will rise first."

Salvation is simple. It's a positive step for us to take. It starts us down a road that only gets better with time.

From *"Faith Through Confession"*

Based on The Word of God as found in

Romans 10:8

"The word is near you, in your mouth and in your heart."

Faith means believing first, and then seeing what Christ will do.

From *"Seeing Is Believing"*

Based on The Word of God as found in

Mark 15:32

"'Let the Christ, the King of Israel, come down now from the cross that we may see and believe.' Those who were crucified with him also reviled him."

When someone proclaims their faith in Christ, that's always a good reason to get together and celebrate.

From *"Celebrating Christ"*

Based on The Word of God as found in

Luke 15:32

"It was fitting to celebrate and be glad, for this your brother was dead, and is alive; he was lost, and is found."

The truth of our endeavors is found in Christ. If we choose another way, our efforts will crumble to dust.

From *"God's Laughter"*

Based on The Word of God as found in

Psalm 2:4

"He who sits in the heavens laughs; the Lord holds them in derision."

God sees the future. To Him it's already come to pass. We wait on Him to bring it to fruition.

From *"God's Perspective"*

Based on The Word of God as found in

Job 30:1

"But now they laugh at me, men who are younger than I, whose fathers I would have disdained to set with the dogs of my flock."

Speaking Jesus is speaking truth, and that's more important than money, houses, and cars could ever be.

From *"Speaking Jesus"*

Based on The Word of God as found in

Luke 16:13-14

"No servant can serve two masters, for either he will hate the one and love the other or he will be devoted to the one and despise the other. You cannot serve God and money. The Pharisees … heard all these things and ridiculed him."

When God speaks, water flows from the rock, and we are satisfied.

From *"Water from the Rock"*

Based on The Word of God as found in

Isaiah 48:21

"They did not thirst when he led them through the deserts;
he made water flow for them from the rock; he split the
rock and the water gushed out."

If we choose to live for Christ, let's make every part of our lives live up to His exacting standard.

From *"The Law of the Land"*

Based on The Word of God as found in

Acts 19:38

"If therefore Demetrius and the craftsmen with him have a complaint against anyone, the courts are open, and there are proconsuls. Let them bring charges against one another."

Our battle cry is sure, for Christ proclaims He brings us the victory.

From *"The Battle Is Already Won"*

Based on The Word of God as found in

Revelation 12:7-8

"Now war arose in heaven, Michael and his angels fighting against the dragon. And the dragon and his angels fought back, but he was defeated, and there was no longer any place for them in heaven."

325

Salvation allows the Christian to become part of God.

From *"Formed from God's Hands"*

Based on The Word of God as found in

1 John 2:27

"But as his anointing teaches you about everything, and is true, and is no lie—just as it has taught you, abide in him."

God calls us to gratitude, for when we're thankful, our quality of attitude lifts us from our despair.

From *"Our Calling from God"*

Based on The Word of God as found in

Deuteronomy 8:7

"For the Lord your God brings you into a good land, a land of brooks of water, of fountains and depths that spring out of valleys and hills."

Our power comes from the Lord, for He is our right hand and our strength.

From *"Our Right Hand of Power"*

Based on The Word of God as found in

Exodus 15:6

"Your right hand, O Lord, glorious in power, your right hand, O Lord, shatters the enemy."

The love that drew us to Christ overflows compassion unto the world.

From *"Softening Our Hearts"*

Based on The Word of God as found in

Mark 4:20

"But those that were sown on the good soil are the ones who hear the word and accept it and bear fruit, thirtyfold and sixtyfold and a hundredfold."

There's no time like the present to step out in faith and live our lives for the Lord.

From *"Our Drink Offering Poured Out"*

Based on The Word of God as found in

2 Timothy 4:6

"For I am already being poured out as a drink offering, and the time of my departure has come."

When we choose to pray, the devil loses, and everyone else gains.

From *"Why Pray?"*

Based on The Word of God as found in

Jeremiah 33:3

"Call to me and I will answer you, and will tell you great and hidden things that you have not known."

Hip, hip, hurrah! Three cheers for Jesus! When we raise our praises unto Him, He is eternally glorified.

From *"Sing a New Song Unto the Great I Am"*

Based on The Word of God as found in

Psalm 33:2

"Give thanks to the Lord with the lyre; make melody to him with the harp of ten strings!"

Jesus is our hope and our indescribable gift. He offers us life, and we find that life through Him.

From *"The Beginnings of Jesus"*

Based on The Word of God as found in

Proverbs 8:26-27

"Before he had made the earth with its fields, or the first of the dust of the world, when he established the heavens, I was there."

When we open our hand in faith, we'll find God offering us the assurance of His eternal presence.

From *"Our Open Hand of Faith"*

Based on The Word of God as found in

Titus 1:2

"In hope of eternal life, which God, who never lies, promised before the ages began."

When we check our spiritual trust meter, let's make sure it reads all the way on the side of Christ.

From *"Checking Our Trust Meter"*

Based on The Word of God as found in

Jeremiah 17:5

"Thus says the Lord: 'Cursed is the man who trusts in man and makes flesh his strength, whose heart turns away from the Lord.'"

When we love those whom we have the right to hate, we've truly taken on the righteous mantle of Christ.

From *"God's Divine Hand"*

Based on The Word of God as found in

Philemon 15-16

"For this perhaps is why he was parted from you for a while, that you might have him back forever, no longer as a bondservant but ... as a beloved brother—especially to me, but how much more to you."

336

We must be happy in all things, both good and bad, so that Christ's message will spread across the world.

From *"Rejoicing in Tribulation"*

Based on The Word of God as found in

Acts 5:41

"Then they left the presence of the council, rejoicing that they were counted worthy to suffer dishonor for the name."

Jesus does for us because He loves us, and He looks for our gratitude to flow back unto Him.

From *"The Right Kind of Worship"*

Based on The Word of God as found in

John 6:15

"Perceiving then that they were about to come and take him by force to make him king, Jesus withdrew again to the mountain by himself."

338

When the joy of Jesus runs in our veins, we won't be able to keep it quiet.

From *"Spreading the Good News"*

Based on The Word of God as found in

John 5:15

"The man went away and told the Jews that it was Jesus who had healed him."

When we take a risk to help those in need, God's love will flow from us unto them.

From *"Which Traveler Are We?"*

Based on The Word of God as found in

Luke 10:30

"Jesus replied, 'A man was going down from Jerusalem to Jericho, and he fell among robbers, who stripped him and beat him and departed, leaving him half dead.'"

When we support those who travel for Christ, we minister with them in the good they do.

From *"Packing Our Traveling Bag"*

Based on The Word of God as found in

Acts 22:21

"And he said to me, 'Go, for I will send you far away to the Gentiles.'"

Today's our day to rock the airwaves with our shout for Christ. We are exalted in Him!

From *"Aiming High for Christ"*

Based on The Word of God as found in

James 1:9

"The man went away and told the Jews that it was Jesus who had healed him."

God navigates us into better and better things through our trust in Him.

From *"Our Fortunate Exchange"*

Based on The Word of God as found in

John 16:7

"Nevertheless, I tell you the truth: it is to your advantage that I go away, for if I do not go away, the Helper will not come to you. But if I go, I will send him to you."

Our trust is in God, for He's written all the parts of the story already, the beginning, the middle, and the end.

From *"God in the Middle"*

Based on The Word of God as found in

John 3:16

"For God so loved the world, that he gave his only Son, that whoever believes in him should not perish but have eternal life."

If we want people around us to find their renewed hope in Christ, first they must be able to find their hope in us.

From *"Renewed Hope in Christ"*

Based on The Word of God as found in

Proverbs 13:12

"Hope deferred makes the heart sick, but a desire fulfilled is a tree of life."

When we get close enough to God, we'll find His truth every time.

From *"Chasing God's Truth"*

Based on The Word of God as found in

Acts 7:33

"Then the Lord said to him, 'Take off the sandals from your feet, for the place where you are standing is holy ground.'"

The fist of God that shakes the heavens also reassures His creation when the storm passes by.

From *"God's Fist Shakes the Heavens"*

Based on The Word of God as found in

Revelation 11:19

"Then God's temple in heaven was opened, and the ark of his covenant was seen within his temple. There were flashes of lightning, rumblings, peals of thunder, an earthquake, and heavy hail."

Our God of today is revealed in the God He was yesterday.

From *"There's No Time Like the, er, Past?"*

Based on The Word of God as found in

Genesis 18:15

"But Sarah denied it, saying, 'I did not laugh,' for she was
afraid. He said, 'No, but you did laugh.'"

348

When our voice fails us, the words of Jesus can fill our lips with success and power.

From *"Repeating the Truth"*

Based on The Word of God as found in

Matthew 21:13

"He said to them, 'It is written, "My house shall be called a house of prayer," but you make it a den of robbers.'"

People see us as we are. If we live in Christ, there'll be no mistaking the salvation we wear.

From *"The Picture We Paint for Christ"*

Based on The Word of God as found in

1 Corinthians 2:4

"My speech and my message were not in plausible words of wisdom, but in demonstration of the Spirit and of power."

We live for Jesus one hour at a time, one thought at a time, in the little moments of every day.

From *"Seven Quick Helps for a Christian Life"*

Based on The Word of God as found in

Jude 1:2

"May mercy, peace, and love be multiplied to you."

When our Christian morals reflect Christ, our lives will reflect His love.

From *"Our Lifestyle in Christ"*

Based on The Word of God as found in

Luke 3:14

"Do not extort money from anyone by threats or by false accusation, and be content with your wages."

Christ still speaks to us through the Word when we open our hearts unto Him.

From *"Open Letter from Christ"*

Based on The Word of God as found in

1 Peter 3:15

"In your hearts honor Christ the Lord as holy, always being prepared to make a defense to anyone who asks you for a reason for the hope that is in you; yet do it with gentleness and respect."

Let's let the world know we love Christ, and that we want others to love Him, too.

From *"Sharing the Good Word"*

Based on The Word of God as found in

Hebrews 4:16

"Let us then with confidence draw near to the throne of grace, that we may receive mercy and find grace to help in time of need."

354

Let's choose to obey God, because, after all, we live in God's House.

From *"The Master of All Things"*

Based on The Word of God as found in

Daniel 4:17

"The sentence is by the decree of the watchers, the decision by the word of the holy ones, to the end that the living may know that the Most High rules the kingdom of men and gives it to whom he will."

When we keep our eyes on Jesus' return, we'll have no trouble keeping our faith in Him firm.

From *"Our Upcoming Victory Celebration"*

Based on The Word of God as found in

Isaiah 26:17

"Like a pregnant woman who writhes and cries out in her pangs when she is near to giving birth, so were we because of you, O Lord."

Let's make sure we're on the right side of the line when the Lord raises His fist to bring down the house of the wicked.

From *"Wrongs Righted by Christ"*

Based on The Word of God as found in

John 5:15

"The Lord knows how to rescue the godly from trials, and to keep the unrighteous under punishment until the day of judgment."

When we come to Christ, we become like Christ, and our goals are no longer the same.

From *"Our Reason for Being"*

Based on The Word of God as found in

Acts 26:18

"To open their eyes, so that they may turn from darkness to light and from the power of Satan to God, that they may receive forgiveness of sins and a place among those who are sanctified by faith in me."

358

We're on the side of Jesus, or we're on the side of the world. Our choice is revealed in the life we choose to live.

From *"Stephen's Defense"*

Based on The Word of God as found in

Act 7:58

"Then they cast him out of the city and stoned him. And the witnesses laid down their garments at the feet of a young man named Saul."

When we cease our doubting, that's when God will start delivering us from the problems that threaten to devour us.

From *"Whose Doubting Will Cease"*

Based on The Word of God as found in

Daniel 6:27

"He delivers and rescues; he works signs and wonders in heaven and on earth, he who has saved Daniel from the power of the lions."

The time to come to Jesus is now, and yesterday, and tomorrow. He's a Savior for all the ages.

From *"A Christ for the Ages"*

Based on The Word of God as found in

2 Corinthians 1:10

"He delivered us from such a deadly peril, and he will deliver us. On him we have set our hope that he will deliver us again."

When the world has us trapped, we can find our freedom through the saving grace of Christ the King.

From *"Released from Our Chains"*

Based on The Word of God as found in

Psalm 35:10

"All my bones shall say, 'O Lord, who is like you, delivering the poor from him who is too strong for him, the poor and needy from him who robs him?'"

If we have Jesus inside, people will see Him shine in everything we do.

From *"Our Ultimate Role Model"*

Based on The Word of God as found in

1 Peter 2:21

"For to this you have been called, because Christ also suffered for you, leaving you an example, so that you might follow in his steps."

Man may question, and he should. Jesus has the answer, and He will. When we choose to listen, we'll find the truth.

From *"Our Jesus Answer"*

Based on The Word of God as found in

Romans 7:24

"Wretched man that I am! Who will deliver me from this body of death?"

When the storms of life knock us to the ground, God will raise us up again, and we will flourish in Him.

From *"Our FRESH God"*

Based on The Word of God as found in

Psalm 17:8

"Keep me as the apple of your eye; hide me in the shadow of your wings."

We hope you enjoyed this set of 365 *Power Quotes*. It's our belief and desire that they will manifest God's presence in your life daily.

Get all the *Power Quotes* books today!

Power Quotes: Unlocking New Levels of Faith in Christ

Power Quotes: Quotes to Release Your Spiritual Success

Power Quotes: Enabling Your Walk with Jesus

Power Quotes: Opening the Power of God's Word

Power Quotes: Revealing God's Path for Your Life

All *Power Quotes* volumes are available at ThreeSkilletPublishing.com and MyChurchNotes.net.

Also available on Amazon.

 THREE SKILLET